EMANUEL SWEDENBORG (1688-1772) is acknowledged as one of the great thinkers of the eighteenth century and a pioneering figure in the history of Western thought. Philosopher, theologian, visionary, scientist and statesman, his book *Heaven and Hell* has had a direct influence on William Blake, Honoré de Balzac, Gérard de Nerval, W B Yeats, S T Coleridge, Fyodor Dostoevsky, C G Jung and many others, and his theory of correspondences is rightly understood as one of the defining influences on Romantic and Symbolist thought. More recently, through the work of Czesław Miłosz, Italo Calvino, A S Byatt and Iain Sinclair, we see his name re-emerge in relation to 'pyschogeography', 'historical realism' and 'magical realism'. Jorge Luis Borges once described him as the most extraordinary man in recorded history. *Introducing Swedenborg* is the first in a series of pocket introductions providing accessible essays on his thought and influence.

PETER ACKROYD is a broadcaster, essayist and one of the UK's foremost biographers and novelists. He has written nearly 40 works of non-fiction, including studies on William Blake, T S Eliot and Isaac Newton, and nearly 20 works of fiction. Among his many awards are the Whitbread Biography Award (1984), the Guardian Fiction Prize (1985) and the James Tait Black Memorial Prize (1998). He was elected a fellow of the Royal Society of Literature in 1984 and was awarded a CBE in 2003.

TITLES IN THE SERIES

Introducing
Swedenborg

Em. Swedenborg.

Introducing
Swedenborg

PETER ACKROYD

The Swedenborg Society
20-21 Bloomsbury Way
London
WC1A 2TH

2021

Typeset at Swedenborg House
Printed at T J Books Limited, Padstow
Introducing Swedenborg © 2021,
Peter Ackroyd/Swedenborg Society

Series/commissioning editor: Stephen McNeilly

Copy editors: Avery Curran and James Wilson

Frontispiece: Portrait of Swedenborg attributed to Edwin Roffe c.1878
Cover and book design © 2021, Stephen McNeilly
Cover image: Paul Gauguin, *Vision of the Sermon*
(Jacob Wrestling with the Angel) © National Galleries of Scotland

Published by:
The Swedenborg Society
Swedenborg House
20-21 Bloomsbury Way
London WC1A 2TH

ISBN: 978-0-85448-220-7
British Library Cataloguing-in-Publication Data.
A catalogue record for this book
is available from the British Library.

Contents

Chronology

1688   Born Emanuel Swedberg on 29 January.

1709   He graduates from Uppsala University and publishes his first work, *Selected Sentences.*

1710   He travels to London and attends lectures by Isaac Newton and studies with Edmond Halley and John Flamsteed. George Berkeley publishes *A Treatise Concerning the Principles of Human Knowledge.*

1714-15 He drafts designs for a series of novel inventions, including a water clock, a submarine and an airplane. King Louis XIV of France dies and is succeeded by his grandson, Louis XV, aged 5. Emanuel publishes three volumes of poetry. G W Leibniz writes *Monadology.*

1716-18 Emanuel is introduced to King Charles XII of Sweden and he publishes Sweden's first scientific journal.

1718 He declines an invitation to become Professor of Astronomy at Uppsala University, Sweden.

1719 The Swedberg family is ennobled and Emanuel's name is changed to Swedenborg. He takes a seat in the Swedish House of Nobles.

1723 Swedenborg's appointment to the role of extraordinary assessor on the Swedish Board of Mines is confirmed.

1724 Swedenborg declines an invitation to succeed Nils Celsius as Professor of Astronomy at Uppsala University.

1726 *Gulliver's Travels* by Jonathan Swift is published.

1727 J S Bach composes *St Matthew Passion*. Isaac Newton dies.

1734 Swedenborg publishes his philosophical and scientific *magnum opus*, *Opera Philosophica et Mineralia* in Leipzig where J S Bach is Musical Director at St Thomas Church. Swedenborg is invited to correspond with the Russian Academy of Sciences.

1736-8 He travels to Paris and Venice to study anatomy and drafts a study of the brain resulting in two large unpublished manuscripts entitled *The Cerebrum* and *The Brain*.

1740-1 He is nominated into the Swedish Academy of Sciences by his cousin Carl Linneaus and publishes *The Economy of the Animal Kingdom* with Voltaire's printer and bookseller François Changuion. In this work he introduces his science of correspondences.

1743 Swedenborg buys a house and plot of land in Hornsgatan, Stockholm. This is the year in which he is first addressed by a spirit.

1743-4 In a private journal, published after his death as the *Journal of Dreams,* Swedenborg describes having a vision of Christ.

1744-5 Swedenborg publishes his *The Animal Kingdom* and *The Worship and Love of God*, and begins a multi-volume study of the Old Testament entitled *The Word Explained*.

1747 He resigns from the Board of Mines. He also begins his *Spiritual Diary* which he continues for nearly 20 years but leaves unpublished.

1748 David Hume publishes *An Enquiry Concerning Human Understanding*.

1749-56 Swedenborg publishes his most important work, an eight-volume biblical exegesis *Arcana Caelestia* which is printed anonymously in London by John Lewis and John Hart.

1753 Carl Linnaeus publishes *Species Plantarum*.

1755 The Lisbon earthquake.

1757 Swedenborg writes of a 'Last Judgment' in the spiritual world. William Blake is born.

1758   Whilst in London, Swedenborg publishes 5
        works printed as supplements to his *Arcana
        Caelestia*. These are: *The Worlds in Space*, *The
        Last Judgment*, *The New Jerusalem*, *The White
        Horse* and his most famous and widely read work
        Heaven and Hell.

1757-9 During this time he also begins a multi-volume
        commentary on the Book of Revelation entitled
        The Apocalypse Explained. He prepares it for the
        press but decides, for reasons still unknown, not
        to publish.

1759   Voltaire publishes *Candide*.

1762   Jean-Jacques Rousseau publishes *Emile,
        or On Education*. Immanuel Kant writes to
        Swedenborg. Swedenborg indicates he will offer a
        reply in a forthcoming work.

1763   In Amsterdam Swedenborg publishes 4 new
        works on the theme of the New Jerusalem and
        a small work on the Last Judgment. *Divine
        Love and Wisdom* is published soon after and is
        thought to be his response to Kant.

1764   Swedenborg publishes *Divine Providence*.

1766   Immanuel Kant publishes his book on
        Swedenborg later translated into English as
        Dreams of a Spirit-Seer. That year Swedenborg
        publishes *The Apocalypse Revealed*.

1767   Premier of Wolfgang Amadeus Mozart's first

opera *Apollo et Hyacinthus*, in Salzburg.

1768   Swedenborg publishes *Conjugial Love* and for the first time puts his name on the title page of his theological works.

1769   In London and Amsterdam he publishes *The Interaction of the Soul & Body* and *Brief Exposition of the Doctrines of the New Church.* A controversy breaks out in Sweden regarding the publication of *Conjugial Love* and his books are confiscated.

1771   Swedenborg travels to Amsterdam and publishes *The True Christian Religion* then travels to London. When in London he suffers from a stroke but partially recovers.

1772   He writes to John Wesley and on Sunday 29 March, Swedenborg dies.

How is it possible that a Swedish gentleman who became an Assessor in the Royal Board of Mines, and whose early essays were concerned among other subjects with metallurgy, hearing aids and longitude, could become a renowned visionary who conversed with angels and spirits?

Emanuel Swedenborg was born in the St James parish of Stockholm on 29 January 1688, a date which, according to the modern calendar, became 9 February. His father, Jesper Swedberg, was a pastor before becoming a professor at Uppsala University and then bishop of Skara, which has its own cathedral and is one of the oldest cities in the country. Like his son he was a prolific and versatile writer. He noted that 'I would be able to fill a wheelbarrow with the books I have written';[1] the most accurate account suggests that he composed more than fifty, among them a Latin-Swedish dictionary and a Swedish grammar. The father was also susceptible to dreams and visions. Of Swedenborg's mother, Sara, much less is known; she seems to have been rich and noted for her composure despite the fact that she gave birth to nine children before her own death in 1696 at the age of thirty. Swedenborg was eight years old when she died, but there is no record of his reaction to her early demise. His older brother, Albrecht, died a few weeks later. The young Emanuel was much acquainted with death.

His father married again in the following year to Sara Bergia, the daughter of a priest and wealthy widow of a judge. According to Jesper she favoured Emanuel among her stepchildren, and Swedenborg himself had happy memories of his childhood. In one of his later works he wrote of the delights of childhood in a manner that suggests memories of his own. Children, he writes:

have no worries about food and clothing, or about the future. They do not look to the world or want a lot from it. They love their parents, their nurses, their child companions with whom they engage in innocent play. They allow themselves to be guided, they listen and obey.[2]

But his young life was not all play. He already experienced visions of children who remained invisible to others; they told him of matters which, when he repeated them to his parents, suggested that he had been allowed glimpses into the spiritual world. He wrote to a friend that:

From my 4th to my 10th year, I was constantly in thought about God, salvation, and man's spiritual suffering.

Several times I disclosed things that amazed my father and mother, who thought that angels must be speaking through me. [3]

But he was also engaged in more practical matters. He realized that by breathing slowly he was able to better concentrate and understand; it was an insight into physiology that he remembered all his life.

There was much to learn.

From the age of seven or eight he began studying Greek and Latin in order to prepare himself for university. He did not have to wait for long; he was admitted to Uppsala University in 1699, at the age of eleven, where he was introduced to Hebrew as well as consolidating his mastery of the classical languages. The lectures on philosophy included Plato and Aristotle and extended to mathematics, astronomy, medicine, history and law. His understanding was assisted by his brother-in-law, Eric Benzelius, with whom he lodged after his parents had moved to the diocese of Skara. Benzelius was the librarian of the university, and a devotee of Descartes, with a passion for education; it was he who fired Swedenborg's passion for mathematics and physics. At this stage of his life he was ambitious and purposeful, but he felt constrained in the student debating societies by a stammer or stutter. In 1709, however, he attained the recognition of his learning with a sixty-two page dissertation on the *Selected Sentences from Publius Syrus the Mime*, a sequence of aphorisms on moral and psychological themes copiously annotated by Swedenborg.

At the end of his university career it was time to move on and to explore the discoveries and conclusions of others in foreign lands. This was, after all, to become known as the Age of Reason or, in less ponderous terms, the Enlightenment. For him, the first port of call was England, the home of the Royal Society and, among others, of Locke and of Newton.

At the end of July 1710 he found berth on a merchant ship and sailed across the North Sea. London became in a sense his spiritual home; he visited, and stayed in, the city on seven different occasions and it was the London hermeticists like William Blake who most warmly embraced him. It is not known if Blake and Swedenborg ever met in the little world of London dissent, but it is possible.

On this first occasion the city was the first stop in a Grand Tour that lasted for four years. He has an immoderate thirst for learning combined with an equally assiduous pursuit of fame. He read Newton and attended lectures at the Royal Society in Crane Court. And he worked with the great English astronomers of the time, Edmond Halley and John Flamsteed, and visited the Royal Greenwich Observatory. He met celebrated mathematicians, geologists, physicians and theologians as well as the famous botanist, Hans Sloane; no doubt they conversed in Latin.

He stayed in London for two and a half years before making his way to Holland and then

travelling on to Paris where he grew sick, the first
of only two occasions when his body failed him.

*

On his return to Sweden in the spring or summer
of 1715 he was filled with ideas, no doubt inspired
by the new acquaintances whom he had met.

He informed his brother-in-law of his proposed
inventions for a water pump, a machine
for lifting heavy objects, a machine gun, a
submarine, a mechanical carriage, a flying
carriage, 'together with several kinds of air guns,
which once loaded could shoot 60 to 70 shots in
succession'.[4] At this stage of his life he was eager
for acclaim, a weakness he did not disown for
some years. In the meantime he began to edit
a journal, *Daedalus Hyperboreus*, filled with
mechanical and scientific matter. The king of
Sweden, Charles XII, was so impressed that he
enlisted Swedenborg as Assessor of Mines; he
remained on the Royal Board of Mines for thirty-
one years. It was the only professional job he ever

had. But in the course of his work he helped to build a series of locks that linked Stockholm to the North Sea, contemplated the construction of saltworks and transported the Swedish navy some fifteen miles across land. He was not a visionary recluse. Partly as a result the new queen ennobled the Swedberg family and in 1719 Emanuel took his place in the House of Nobles. This was the year after the death of Charles XII, and the demise of *Daedalus Hyperboreus*.

Yet even as he continued his active life in the world he became preoccupied with the spiritual world from which he knew he derived his insights and his writing. From 1724 to 1734 he ceased to publish, largely because he was engaged in a three-volume work entitled *Opera Philosophica et Mineralia* (*Philosophical and Mineralogical Works*). The last two volumes were treatises on the properties of tin and copper, but the first of them came as a surprise or, for some, a revelation.

How did the infinite, which is not material and is not defined by time or space, give rise to

the finite? He posits the existence of a number of
points without dimension, which emerge from
the infinite and which are the cause of matter.
Every point is in turn filled with infinite energy.
He added that:

> *we are at the same time bound to suppose,*
> *that in the producing cause there was*
> *something of a will that it should be*
> *produced; something of an active quality,*
> *which produced it; and something of an*
> *intelligent nature, determining that it*
> *should be produced in such a manner…*
> *in a word, something infinitely intelligent,*
> *infinitely provident, infinitely active, and*
> *infinitely productive.* [5]

How do these points manifest themselves? They
are constantly in the state of becoming since
'being kept in being is constant coming into
being'.[6] They take the perfect form of the spiral,
'continual, eternal circles from the centre to

the periphery, without limit, end, or angle'.[7]
The nebulae form spirals, and the planets
spiral around the sun, tokens of the ineffable
beginnings of matter. So there was a moment
when the planet on which we live, and the
solar system of which we are a part, were a
manifestation of the infinite. For Swedenborg
the infinite was an aspect of the deity, 'For
without the utmost devotion to the Supreme
Being, no one can be a complete and truly
learned philosopher'.[8]

It should be remembered also that in this
period science was considered to be part of
philosophy since 'the love of wisdom', the
meaning of philosophy, covered all aspects
of human knowledge. This first volume of
Philosophical and Mineralogical Works marks
Swedenborg's first attempt to understand the
non-material world. But he had come to realize
that philosophy without spiritual understanding
is hollow.

*

In 1735 Swedenborg's father, Jesper Swedberg, died and after a period of mourning he embarked upon another continental journey; this pattern of travel and return would endure for the rest of his life.

In July 1736 he set off for Rome by way of Paris, Venice and Bologna. He began a series of studies on the brain, which were further exploration of his major work on the human soul; he entitled them *The Cerebrum* and *The Brain*, but left them unpublished. In these treatises he draws an analogy between the brain and respiration and explores the existence of cerebrospinal fluid as well as the path of the spinal cord. At a later date he affirmed that the geography of the human body reflected that of heaven, and that the spinal cortex was the avenue through which divine love entered the soul.[9]

In 1740 he stopped in Amsterdam and published part I of another compendious work, *Oeconomia Regni Animalis* or *The Economy of the Animal Kingdom*, in which he looked inwards rather than to the outer whirling stars in order to understand the function and meaning of the human soul. By the 'animal' he meant the animating principle; *anima* in Latin can be translated as 'life' or 'soul'. He published part II in 1741. He then returned back to Sweden in 1742 and continued his studies of anatomy and the brain.

Not long after this period, and when resident in London, he suffered a nervous collapse about which he wrote:

> *In the morning when I woke up, there came again upon me such a swoon or* deliquium *as I had six or seven years ago in Amsterdam* [. . .] *but it was much more subtle, so that I seemed to be near death.* [10]

This was the period when he was writing *Regnum Animale* or *The Animal Kingdom*.

On waking from this near-death experience, he believed that he had achieved better concentration and understanding. He comprehended the nature of blood, for example, which 'meant heavenly things, and in the highest sense means the Lord's Human Essence, and so Love itself'.[11]

These are abstruse matters and in the second part of *The Economy of the Animal Kingdom*, which he had published in 1741, he tried to elucidate his thoughts by means of a series of steps from lower to higher which he called 'correspondences'. This was an occult maxim which had been used elsewhere, namely 'that which is above is like that which is below'. This was the divining principle of his early studies. He affirmed that 'what is natural cannot in any sense come into being without a cause prior to itself. Its cause exists in that which is spiritual'.[12] He had already intuited the truth of this in his writings on the human body, but he would not claim to be its sole progenitor. Something else happened at this time. He was called to his sacred vocation 'in the year 1743; when He opened my sight into the spiritual world, and enabled me to converse with spirits and angels'. [13] This can be construed as the source and origin of his later writings where, for example, he speaks of heaven and hell and converses with their inhabitants.

It was no coincidence that Swedenborg began his *Journal of Dreams* in 1743. Certain pages were later removed, and the rest of the diary comprised some 142 pages. It was not published until 1859, since the erotic and mystical tenor of much of the writing was liable to be rejected as the work of a madman. Yet he was not considered so by those contemporaries who worked and conversed with him; he was still Assessor of Mines, a member of the nobility in the Swedish parliament or Diet, and a colleague of the most prominent scientists and statesmen of the day. He could hardly have been considered insane.

The first entries of the *Journal of Dreams* are typical of any diary, detailing his journeys

and meetings with contemporaries. But there
is a change in the spring of 1744. There are
specifically sexual references, albeit of an
unusual nature. In April 1744 he dreamed that
he 'Lay with one that was by no means pretty,
but still I liked her. She was made like others; I
touched her there, but found that at the entrance
it was set with teeth'.[14] The image of *vagina
dentata* recurs, suggesting a fear of, or aversion
to, sex. Certainly any sexual life he might have
experienced now came to an end. His work was
an all-consuming fire.

In the same month, on 6 April, he recorded
a quite different experience, which was not a
dream but a vision. He writes that he went to
sleep about midnight or later, and was seized
by a 'strong shivering' from his head to his feet.
Words were then 'put into my mouth' which
began with an appeal to 'Oh, thou almighty Jesus
Christ'. He clasped his hands in prayer but 'a
hand emerged, which pressed my hands firmly'.
At the same moment he found himself 'sitting

in his bosom [. . .] He was smiling at me, and I was convinced that he looked like this when he was alive. He spoke to me and asked if I have a health certificate'.[15] This odd reference no doubt alludes to Swedenborg's experience on an earlier journey when a certificate was necessary to prove that he was free of the plague. It is an allusion that somehow lends credence to his vision. He replied, 'Lord, thou knowest better than I'. To which Christ said, 'Well then, do!' The words are mysterious, but Swedenborg interpreted them as 'Do love me' or 'Do as promised'.[16] So here was a man who spoke directly to Christ or God, who spoke with the dead, and who saw visions of spiritual life all around him.

*

Some of these dreams, or visions, or hypnagogic images, marked turning points in Swedenborg's life, even if they were sometimes not clear even to him. Yet it is plain enough that he believed himself to live in eternity.

In May 1744 Swedenborg returned to London from The Hague and took lodgings with a watchmaker, John Paul Brockmer, a Moravian who lived in Salisbury Court near the Moravian chapel in Fetter Lane. Brockmer is supposed to have related an encounter in which Swedenborg 'looked very frightful: his hair stood upright, and he foamed a little at his mouth'. In the course of his distracted speech he claimed 'that he was the Messiah: that he was come to be crucified for the Jews'.[17]

It does not seem likely that Swedenborg claimed to be the Messiah. He was known to be a gentle and polite man who did not engage in controversy. It is more likely that the clockmaker misinterpreted some of the more startling or unexpected anecdotes of Swedenborg's spiritual life. Brockmer was a Moravian, and for a time Swedenborg consorted with the members of the Moravian church who professed a fundamentalist Protestantism. It seems possible that he considered joining them.

One incident can stand for many in this period of spiritual uncertainty. In September 1744 he was contemplating a problem when he heard a voice saying 'Hold your tongue or I will strike you'.[18] The meaning may be that he was writing too much. Another entry in a journal for April 1745 relates to this visit to London:

At mid-day, about dinner time, an angel who was with me spoke to me saying that I was not to indulge the belly too much at table.

He described the appearance of this angel as resembling 'a vapour exuding from the pores of my body like something watery' which then slipped down onto the floor where it became 'various little worms' which were burned up with a fiery light and with a sound of thunder.[19]

In a later version of the same mystical experience the angel becomes an old man who appears suddenly before Swedenborg in an inn and counselled him to 'Eat not so much' before disappearing into blackness. Swedenborg hastened back to his lodgings when the man once more appeared and announced that he was the Lord and Saviour who had chosen him for a special task.

Swedenborg believed this to be a defining moment in his spiritual life. He told a friend:

> *that same night also were opened to me, so that I became thoroughly convinced of their reality, the worlds of spirits, heaven, and hell, and I recognized there many acquaintances of every condition in life. From that day I gave up the study of all worldly science, and laboured in spiritual things, according as the Lord commanded me to write. Afterwards the Lord opened, daily very often, my bodily eyes, so that, in the middle of the day I could see into the other world, and in a state of perfect wakefulness converse with angels and spirits.* [20]

It was the fullest elucidation of his mission on earth. On one occasion he was disturbed by a friend in the course of a vision; he was discovered in a rigid posture, as if in a trance. He came to his normal senses gradually but he still seemed to be bewildered and walked forward uncertainly.[21]

For a while he continued work on *The Animal Kingdom*, but he never completed it. On the night of 8 October, after he had since taken lodgings with another Moravian from the Fetter Lane chapel, he had a vision of 'the most beautiful garden that can be imagined' from which he entered a long chamber 'where beautiful white vessels of milk and bread were'. His most recent biographer has suggested that the garden was for him an image 'of his concept of the nature of true literary work', and a few weeks later Swedenborg himself interpreted a similar vision as referring 'to all the work I now enter upon in the name of God'.[22]

*

In the autumn of 1744 Swedenborg stopped
his work on *The Animal Kingdom* and began
an account entitled *De Cultu et Amore Dei* or
The Worship and Love of God. This also was
never completed but in the early months of
1745 he published the first two parts of what
he had written. It was his most comprehensive
attempt to elucidate the spiritual meaning and
intention of the Bible by means of allegory and
revelation. It might be considered as a verse
epic in prose; scholars have identified his use
of ornate Latin and he confessed to 'making a
playful use of the Latin language',[23] perhaps
to differentiate it from the sober Latin of his
technical treatises. It was also the beginning
of his more comprehensive study of the Bible
that occupied him for two years and which, in
English translation, under the title *The Word
Explained*, covers eight volumes.

In *The Worship and Love of God*, however,
he meditated upon the first two chapters of

Genesis that deal with Creation and the spiritual
significance of Adam and Eve. He would never
claim full understanding of the text. 'Seek no
more for the source', he wrote, 'since you are in
its very innermost [. . .] Fill your understanding
with all that is good from this gushing spring'.[24]
Coleridge was highly impressed by one of the
many footnotes that explain Swedenborg's
conclusions on the formation of the firmament;
he commented that 'Note (b) would of itself
suffice to mark Swedenborg as a man of
philosophic *genius*, radicative and evolvent'.[25]

The new created world is as a garden
populated by plants and animals, but it is not
finished until the appearance of Adam who is
an image of the human soul. He is instructed
by angelic messengers about the nature and
meaning of God's desire to create the animal,
vegetable and mineral worlds.

This description has been interpreted as a
compendium of the beliefs that Swedenborg
has already divulged or would come to explain.

Adam himself is as a little child and Swedenborg commented later that 'a person begins to become wise who knows little, virtually nothing from himself as the source. This is the same as to say that he who is nothing is something [. . .] It is then that the Lord is with him for the first time [. . .] his wisdom is then not his own'.[26] Adam is joined by heavenly creatures, who are feminine, who tell him that 'Nothing flows out from you, but all things stream forth from the highest'.[27]

The first man is taught that good and evil are spiritual forces that strive for mastery in a battle that persists through the ages of the world. But then Adam is made aware of Christ's ultimate coming, and the angelic powers of wisdom leave him with a promise that 'We perfect your mind. Therefore, through us you are [God's] image. We behold your love with our eyes, and through us you may also see him'.[28]

The first two parts of the book were published in the early months of 1745, and he was now ready to devote himself to theological writing and to abandon that search for reputation or worldly position that had partly motivated his practical work on mechanics. In 1747, as he became immersed in biblical studies, he resigned his position as Assessor of Mines much to the regret of his colleagues on the Board of Mines who were ready to promote him. He began to refresh his knowledge of Hebrew, and drew up an index of the biblical texts and of the passages that prophesy the coming of the Messiah.

From 1745 he kept a journal to which he added material for the next twenty years; these were notes that included his dreams, visions, ideas and revelations, which were also written in Latin and which he may have collected for future publication. One of his early editors called them *The Spiritual Diary* and a more recent one entitled them *Spiritual Experiences*. He did not publish them, but he drew material from them for his later work, and even provided an index for the ready location of passages. He knew very well the source from which they came. He wrote that:

*I can solemnly swear that for the space of
eight months now I have by the pure mercy
and grace of the Messiah been having the
same sort of conversation with people in
heaven as with my friends on earth
[. . .] namely from the middle of 1745 to
January 29, 1746.* [29]

What had been fortuitous or occasional now
seems to have become a continuing dialogue
between earth and heaven.

*I have spoken with heavenly beings,
with spirits, and with the dead who have
risen, even with those who said they were
Abraham, Isaac, Jacob, Esau, Rebecca,
Moses, Aaron, and the Apostles, especially
with Paul and James.* [30]

These renowned spirits dictated much of what
he wrote or, rather, 'were totally guiding my
hand, and so it was they who were writing'.[31] The

consequences became clear when Swedenborg began to publish again in 1749, with a series of eight volumes entitled *Arcana Coelestia* or *Secrets of Heaven*. The publisher was John Lewis of 1, Paternoster Row near St Paul's Cathedral; the Row was lined with bookshops, and was the centre of London's publishing industry. The publisher, or a sympathetic reader, announced that 'This Work is intended to be such an exposition of the whole Bible as was never attempted in any language before'.[32]

The advertisement would not have been included without the author's consent. But despite Swedenborg's ambition of 'making known the spiritual contents of Scripture'[33] he managed only to interpret Genesis and Exodus. His close reading of the Bible was not foreshortened, however, and he came to rely upon it until the end of his life. He had begun his contemplation with the reading of John's Revelation but, with the exception of his *Apocalypse Revealed* printed in 1766, he only alluded to his loving attachment to that text in *Vera Christiana Religio*, or *The True Christian Religion*, published in 1771. His most splendid account of Revelation, written from 1757 to 1759 in six volumes, was not published until after his death.

*

In the spring of 1750, a year after the publication of the first volume of *Arcana*, Swedenborg returned to Stockholm where he redeveloped a house and planted a garden. The summerhouse still survives and is preserved in the Skånsen Museum Park of the capital. One of his friends, Carl Robsahm, has described the property as 'about a stone's throw in length and breadth', which is not very precise. He adds that 'The rooms of his dwelling house were small and plain enough'.[34]

On his desk he kept no books except for the Bible in Hebrew and Greek as well as his handwritten index of his own books. His library was kept in a garden pavilion, together with gardening tools. Robsahm goes on to detail the visionary's habits of life. 'Swedenborg worked day and night and never had fixed hours for work or rest. "When I am sleepy", he said, "I go to bed"'.[35]

His domestic servant was the gardener's wife, and her main duties consisted of making his bed and leaving a large jug of water in an anteroom so that he could make the coffee, which he drank continually. His midday meal, and his evening supper, consisted of a wheat loaf bun soaked in skimmed milk.

From autumn to early spring he kept a fire in his stove, partly to brew the coffee he required. There was no fire in his bedroom, however, and when he slept he covered himself with three or four blankets.

His living room was 'neat and tidy, yet sombre'. It contained a marble table, which he bequeathed to the Royal Board of Mines. He was never elegantly dressed but in winter wore a coat of reindeer skin with the hairy side turned

inwards and in summer a 'robe'. He was forgetful
in sartorial matters and, if not inspected by the
maid, would wear odd combinations of dress.
One shoe buckle might be made of gems, for
example, and the other of silver.[36]

He spoke slowly, as a result of his stutter, and
as his reputation grew he became more reserved.
There was talk of his visions throughout the
city, and he was sometimes derided as mad.
But he kept his equanimity and was always
cheerful and friendly; he welcomed friends and
acquaintances and in particular took delight
in their children who played in his garden.
He rarely went to church, largely because he
disliked the sermons which must have seemed to
him to be irrelevant.

He was hardly ever ill but he was plagued by
toothache. There was no point in consulting
a dentist, however, since he believed that the
discomfort was 'caused by the influx of hell
from canting hypocrites who tempted him, and
who by correspondences caused this pain'.[37] By

this he meant that the spiritual world affected the material world.

The gardener and his wife sometimes heard him cry out in the night. When they asked him on the following morning if anything was wrong he replied that 'evil spirits had been permitted to abuse him, and that he had responded and been indignant with them'.[38] On one occasion he remained in bed for several days, groaning, but then suddenly recovered his cheerfulness. He knew that the Lord would not tempt him beyond what he could bear.

Robsahm once asked the maid how he seemed on these occasions, and she recalled that one afternoon she entered his room, 'and when she opened the door, the pupils of his eyes had the appearance of the brightest fire'. She cried out in fear but he asked her to be calm since 'the Lord has opened my bodily eyes, and I have been in the spirit; but in a little while, I shall be all right again; and this does me no harm'. He had a habit of saying 'well! well!' and 'good! good!'[39]

*

It had taken him seven years fully to publish his close reading of Genesis and Exodus in *Arcana Caelestia* in which he wrote of Adam and of the Tree of Life, which was an image of Adam's happiness. He described the birth of Eve, and interpreted it as dividing the physical union of love and wisdom. The Tree of Life was accompanied by the Tree of Knowledge, but the eating of the apple symbolized that the unity with God was lost.

> *Men's desire to probe into mysteries of faith by means of sensory evidence and factual knowledge was not only the cause of the downfall of the Most Ancient Church [. . .] it is also the cause of the downfall of every Church. For that desire leads not only to falsities but also to evils of life.* [40]

The Fall thus instigated a new era which is symbolized by the second Church, the Noachian

Church. In the first Ancient Church there was an unmediated spiritual communion with the Lord, but the second church lost its connection with the living God and relied upon the efforts of the outer man and the belief in custom and tradition. Reason and logic, with the companionship of conscience, became the governing factors of the spiritual world.

There then came the third age of what Swedenborg called 'the Judaic church'; wisdom is occluded and replaced by ritual and formulae, when all that is holy is veiled and protected in shrines. This in turn was replaced by the Christian age which, having become compromised, continued to the present time, until the New Church announced by Swedenborg came to destroy the old dispensation. 'Then He who sat on the throne said, "Behold, I make all things new". And He said to me, "Write, for these words are true and faithful"'.[41] This was Swedenborg's testament. But the publication of *Arcana* did not mark the termination or fulfilment of his labours.

He travelled to London once more where
no doubt he resumed his acquaintance with
the radical sects which were prevalent in the
late eighteenth century. But he did not visit
the city only. In a heightened state of spiritual
consciousness, which could take the form of
trance, dream or vision, he travelled to heaven
and to hell.

Heaven and Hell, as well as *The White Horse*,
were published in London in 1758. The first
of them has become the most popular of his
writings, largely because of the enormity of its
themes but also because it is written in simple
fashion as if it were a traveller's tale.

In the first section Swedenborg asserts that 'it
has been granted to me to associate with angels
and to talk with them as man with man'; but
there was a distinction in heaven since the angels
speak 'from the thought, for there they have a
cogitative speech or thought speaking'.[42] The
nearest equivalent might be telepathy. He reveals
also that 'angels are unable to utter a single

word of human language [. . .] because they can
utter nothing except what is in entire agreement
with their affections'. Yet they seem to understand
it because 'I have heard angels disclosing the
character of another's life merely from hearing
him speak'.[43] Whether the other is man or angel
is not clear, but the same faculty of interpretation
no doubt applies. Their language can only
properly be interpreted by those who understand
'correspondences' such as, for example, 'love
being the fire of the sun and the truth therefrom
as light from the sun'.[44] Writing in the highest
heaven consists of curves and distinct forms;
good is distributed through the vowels 'u', 'o' and
'a' while truth is conveyed by 'e' and 'i'.[45] 'On
occasion', he says:

> *I have been assigned to the state in which*
> *angels were, and* [. . .] *have talked*
> *with them. At such times I understood*
> *everything. But when I was sent back*
> *into my earlier state* [. . .] *and wanted to*

recall what I had heard, I could not. For there were thousands of things that had no equivalent in concepts of natural thought, that were therefore inexpressible except simply through shiftings of a heavenly light—not at all by human words. [46]

In similar fashion they 'can say more in a minute than many can say in half an hour. They can also set down in a few words the contents of many written pages'. [47] Their thought takes the form of waves.

Each angel is different from another but there are two broad categories in the celestial angels, who understand divine truth in its highest and most interior essence, and the spiritual angels who understand it in a less exalted fashion. The speech of spiritual angels flows in the manner of a gentle stream, while the speech of the celestial angels is energetic and distinct. The Lord appears in the celestial kingdom as a sun, and in the spiritual kingdom as a moon. There are in fact many societies in heaven in which dwell different types of angel. Those who have a clear perception of the divine inhabit the east, for example, while those with more obscure understanding dwell in the west. The light of heaven changes in accordance with the nature of the angels. Nevertheless 'an entire angelic society sometimes appears as a one in the form of an angel, as I have been enabled by the Lord to see'.[48]

There is also more inclusive spiritual truth since 'all the heavens with their societies resemble one man they therefore call heaven the grand and divine man'. So it is that 'Since the whole heaven resembles one man, and is a Divine spiritual man in the greatest form in its very likeness, so heaven, like a man, is arranged into members and parts which are similarly named'.[49] Here Swedenborg touches upon the central image of mystical and cabbalistic devotion exemplified by others, like William Blake who depicts the Divine Man with his arms outstretched in *Albion Rose*.

That is the truth behind Swedenborg's declaration that:

> *angels as to their form are wholly men, having faces, eyes, ears, bodies, arms, hands and feet, and they see and hear one another and talk together* [. . .] *I have seen them in their own light which exceeds by many degrees the noonday light of the world*[.][50]

The fact that God appears in a divine angelic form that is human cannot be understood by those who believe that the Lord is an invisible force and that the spiritual world is wholly divorced from material reality, for the smallest thing in the world has its spiritual counterpart. The breast signifies charity, the loins and organs of generation signify conjugial love, the arms and hands signify the power of truth, the feet signify the natural, the eyes signify understanding, the nostrils signify perception,

the ears signify obedience and the kidneys signify
the scrutiny and correction of truth. [51]

These correspondences apply to the animal
world, too, so that, for example:

> *cattle and their young correspond to the*
> *affections of the natural mind, sheep and*
> *lambs to the affections of the spiritual*
> *mind, while winged creatures, according to*
> *their species, correspond to the intellectual*
> *things of either mind.* [52]

Yet in heaven there is no extension of space
as in the world, and there is no concept of time,
except in so far as daylight is heavenly love and
night is hell. 'Time there is not measured in days,
weeks, or years, but in changes of state'. [53] Space
is irrelevant, since distance is measured only by
the nearness of God; he declares that in heaven,
wherever the angels may happen to be, they are
always facing God. Swedenborg often draws upon
what he calls 'the evidence of experience', as, for

example, those occasions when he has spoken to angels in their dwellings that 'are precisely like the dwellings on earth which are called houses, but more beautiful'.[54] They contain chambers, inner rooms and bedrooms while their gardens include flower beds and lawns. The houses themselves are in close proximity so that they resemble a city 'with streets, roads and public squares'.[55] In the surrounding landscape are mountains, hills, rocks and valleys which are also inhabited by angels of different dispositions. Some angels are naked because nakedness corresponds with innocence.

Swedenborg deals with the matter of mortal death. At that moment the spirit of a person first enters the world of spirits as an exact resemblance of themselves in face and in tone of voice. Subsequently, however, their face is changed according to their inner affections. In the same fashion their habitations change. Those who have devoted themselves to learning for the sake of worldly reputation, for example, 'love sandy places, which they choose in preference to fields and gardens, because sandy places correspond to such studies'. [56]

Swedenborg's vision of hell is to be understood by his maxim that 'for every good there is an opposite evil'. All those in hell 'are ruled by means of their fears' while 'the punishments in hell are manifold, lighter or more severe in accordance with the evils'. [57] Each person believes that they act through their own choice; so it is that a person is the cause of their own evil and so casts themself 'into hell from death, and not the Lord'. [58]

When a person first enters the spiritual realm after death they are met by angels who try to instruct them in the truth, but soon enough the person seeks to get away from the angels' company as it is displeasing to them. 'As soon as the angels perceive this they leave'. Instead the person associates with those spirits who are like them and embrace their own evils. They cast themselves into hell by their own volition 'with the head downwards and the feet upwards'. [59]

The person is greeted with friendliness at first, but the other spirits of hell begin to question them and explore their life 'in respect of his astuteness and consequent ability'.[60] Some are drawn ever deeper as a result, and are confronted by more malignant spirits who treat them with crueller and crueller punishments until they are reduced to the condition of a slave.

All these spirits eventually come to resemble 'the form of their evil'; some have faces like corpses while others burn like torches. Many faces in hell are:

> *disfigured with pimples, warts, and ulcers; many seem to have no face, but in its stead something hairy or bony; and with some only the teeth are seen; their bodies also are monstrous; and their speech is like the speech of anger, hatred, or revenge.*[61]

And yet to themselves, and to each other, they seem normal. The principal evil is self-love. Some protest their innocence while others seek their enemies in order to destroy them. The lust of doing evil is what is known as 'fire' in the Scriptures.

Hell is the demonic opposite of heaven. It has many societies and many neighbourhoods according to the nature of the sin. So we may talk of hells rather than of hell. Just as heat from the sun in heaven flows into shrubberies and beds of flowers, into vegetation and sweet odours, so the sun in hell flows 'into excrementitious and decaying substances produc[ing] putrefactions'.[62] When the hells are opened, there is an appearance of fire with smoke but the inhabitants feel only the warmth they knew in the world. The light of heaven is 'thick darkness to them'.[63] Some hells resemble ruined cities, while others are 'rude huts' with streets and lanes in which the infernal spirits continually quarrel and fight. 'In some of the hells there are nothing but brothels, disgusting to the sight and filled with every kind of filth and excrement'.[64] Swedenborg's account comes to an end shortly after, completing one of the most significant and interesting episodes of his visionary life.

Yet this spiritual life was copious and abundant. After completing *Heaven and Hell* he embarked upon a series of smaller works on the Last Judgment and on the 'new Jerusalem' in which he describes the New Church to which he had earlier testified. It is in some sense a summary of what he had already written but it includes moral as well as visionary concerns; there are small chapters, for example, 'On Baptism', 'On Conscience', 'On the Holy Supper' and 'Of the Church and State'. 'On Providence' states clearly one of his themes. He writes that:

> *Divine Providence pays no attention to what swiftly passes and comes to an end when a person's life in the world ceases, but rather to what lasts for ever, and so has no end. That which has no end is; that which has an end is comparatively non-existent.*[65]

The Worlds in Space was also published in 1758, in which Swedenborg affirms that there is human and intelligent life elsewhere in the universe and, in particular, in the solar system. He converses with the dead from the other worlds, and learns that the inhabitants of Jupiter frequently wash and cleanse their faces and carefully protect them from the heat of the sun. They have a bluish covering made from the bark or cork of a tree that they put around their heads to shield their faces. The 'sole interest' of those from Mercury is 'in gathering information'. 'As soon as they reached me, they searched my memory to see what I knew'. Swedenborg relates that 'They grasped and evaluated what they heard with the same quickness with which they spoke, saying, "Yes, that's right" or "No, that's not correct". They made up their minds almost instantly'. [66] Some other beings appeared to him:

Their faces were not unattractive, but were longer than the faces of other spirits.

*They were about as tall as seven-year-old
children, but of sturdier build, so they
were little people. I was told by some angels
that they were from the Moon.* [67]

There is much more of the same nature, which
still remains of extraordinary interest.

*

More texts followed, including *Divine Love
and Wisdom* in 1763 and *Divine Providence*
in the following year. They are essentially a
restatement and elaboration of Swedenborg's
doctrines, sometimes in aphoristic form. So, for
example, we read that 'there is in all the heavens
no other idea of God than the idea of a Man'
and that 'there is a correspondence of the will
with the heart, and of the understanding with
the lungs'. [68] In these two years seven new works
were printed in Amsterdam to complement his
earlier writings, but in August 1764 he returned
to Stockholm.

By now the range and volume of his doctrines had attracted notice throughout Europe. His succeeding work, *The Apocalypse Revealed,* was written by divine command. He wrote later that 'I heard a voice from heaven saying, "Go to your room and close the door. Get down to the work you started on the Book of Revelation. Carry it to completion within two years"'.[69] And so he did. *The Apocalypse Revealed* was published in 1766.

But Swedenborg was a clairvoyant as well as a visionary. In this period he had at least three revelatory insights that were witnessed by friends or contemporaries. After one of his visits to England, in 1759, he called on a prominent merchant in Gothenburg where he was expecting to dine. Suddenly he left the room and, on returning in obvious dismay, announced that a great fire had erupted in south Stockholm and was spreading quickly; the house of a friend had already been destroyed and his own house was in danger from the conflagration. Gothenburg was 743 kilometres from Stockholm, and of course he could not have been informed in any conventional way.

Two hours later, at eight o'clock in the evening, he left the room again and, when he re-entered, he said 'Thank God! The fire is extinguished, the third door from my house'.[70] When a messenger arrived from Stockholm, a few days later, he confirmed every detail of Swedenborg's report. The fire had started at the precise moment when Swedenborg left the room, and was finally extinguished at eight o'clock. Soon the news of his exact and explicit vision was widely reported, and his fame increased the faith in his visionary writings.

The second report of his clairvoyance concerned the widow of the Dutch ambassador, Madame de Marteville. She was being asked to pay for a silver tea service, at a sum of twenty-five thousand guilders, but she was convinced that her late husband had paid for it before his death. But she could not find the receipt. Knowing Swedenborg's reputation, she visited him and asked for help by any means. He promised to assist her if it was within his power. By means of contemplation he encountered the ambassador in the spirit world and explained to him the dilemma of his former wife. De Marteville told him that he would locate the receipt and resolve the problem. Some days later de Marteville appeared to his wife in a dream and told her that she should look behind a drawer in his desk. 'My child', he said, 'you are worried about the receipt. Just pull out the drawer of my desk all the way [. . .] the receipt was probably pushed back and is lying behind it'.[71] She followed his instructions and came upon the receipt together with a hairpin which she thought to be lost. On the following day Swedenborg called on Madame de Marteville; he must have known what had happened because he told her that he had tried to converse again with her dead husband, but that he did not wish to speak and was travelling to another part of heaven.

The third episode of clairvoyance was involved with the queen of Sweden, Louisa Ulrika. Swedenborg, now a distinguished figure in his country, was invited to a court reception in the autumn of 1761. The queen took him to one side and asked him whether it was true that he could communicate with the dead. He replied:

I cannot converse with all, but with such as I have known in this world; with all royal and princely persons, with all renowned heroes, or great and learned men, whom I have known, either personally or from their actions or writings; consequently of all of whom I could form an idea; for it may be supposed that a person whom I never knew, or of whom I could form no idea, I neither could nor would wish to speak with. [72]

No doubt intrigued by his answer she gave him a question which he should pose to her dead brother, Augustus Wilhelm, prince of Prussia. He accepted the request and soon departed. Three weeks later, he returned to court in order to speak with the queen. She was playing cards at the time and told him that he could speak openly before her companions. He demurred, however, and intimated that he had to speak privately to her. She took him to another chamber, with a courtier in attendance. Here he told her that her brother had sent his blessing and also his apologies for not answering her letter. But he himself had been given the answer by him to repeat to her, and he whispered it to her. The queen was shaken by his words; she turned pale and stepped backwards. 'No one, except God', she said, 'knows this secret'.[73]

*

His life in the world continued, and from 1760 to 1762 he participated in the Swedish parliament, the Diet, until it was suspended by uncertainty in foreign relations when Sweden, one of the allies of France in the Seven Years' War, was close to defeat. He even wrote a paper condemning the excessive printing of money by the Government to subsidize its war expenditure. He did not return to the parliament in 1765, but he may have attended its closing in 1766. In that year, too, he travelled to England where he presented a tract on the calculation of longitude to the Royal Society. It was rejected, however, in favour of a proposal by an Englishman, John Harrison, to measure longitude by means of a marine chronometer.

He was not otherwise engaged in material affairs, with the publication of shorter texts such as *The Divine Love and Wisdom* in 1763, *Divine Providence* in 1764 and *The Apocalypse Revealed* in 1766. But the major work of this period was published in 1768 under the title of *Conjugial Love*. It was the first of his theological works that carried his name on the title page. It aroused more controversy than he could have anticipated, however, and even brought two of his followers close to an accusation of heresy.

He rejected the conventional supposition that celibacy is far holier than sexuality. He asserted that 'Chastity cannot be attributed to people who have renounced marriage by vowing perpetual celibacy unless some true love of marriage remains alive within them'.[74] He celebrates marriage as a union of goodness and truth, and declares that it should be a partnership of equals; this of course directly opposed the orthodox belief that the male was somehow superior to the female. Their unison in harmony was so sacred that it would continue after death where their conjunction would show them to be one angel.

Those who are in love truly conjugial [. . .]
*when they become angels, return into
their youth and adolescence* [. . .] *Each
conjugial partner returns into the prime
of life and into the joys of the age in which*

conjugial love begins to intensify life with
new delights, and to inspire with joyous
activity for the sake of prolification. [75]

This is, in one interpretation, a paean to the delights of sex.

Swedenborg adds that 'from marriages in the heavens, although married partners are there united as on earth, children are not born, but instead of children, goods and truths, and thence wisdom'.[76] He spoke of his encounter with one such partner who took him into the bedroom, on the walls of which were many works of art together with images made of silver. 'What are these?' he asked. The husband answered that 'Some represent the unity of souls, some the conjunction of minds, some the concord of hearts, and some the delights arising therefrom'.[77] Swedenborg himself never married and it is possible that he himself never experienced the sexual delights about which he writes. There was one occasion when he spoke of once having a 'maîtresse', or mistress, but that could mean anything or nothing.[78]

By this time Swedenborg, now aged eighty, had attracted a loyal group of disciples who may be called Swedenborgians. In 1769 he made another journey to London where the air of spiritual radicalism was for him purer than that of continental Europe. Many of the London tracts and pamphlets sold in the bookshops and on the bookstalls were concerned with occult and cabbalistic beliefs. Late eighteenth-century London was awash with mysticism and millenarianism, finding its adversary in the urban preoccupation with commerce and power. In that city he found two men who might be considered his 'disciples', a Quaker and a clergyman from the Church of England, William Cookworthy and Thomas Hartley. They were both involved in the publication and dissemination of some of Swedenborg's writings.

A Swedish priest who was living in London, Arvid Ferelius, often visited him in his lodgings.

Swedenborg also came to his house in 13 Princes Square, close to the Swedish church where he would one day be buried. Swedenborg told Ferelius that he could obtain no peace in that church 'by reason of the spirits, who gainsaid what the preacher laid down, especially when he mentioned three persons in the Divinity, which, in fact, was just like three Gods'.[79]

In a letter written a few years after Swedenborg's death Ferelius described his life in the city:

> *Some one might think that Assessor Swedenborg was eccentric and whimsical; but the very reverse was the case. He was very easy and pleasant in company, talked on every subject that came up, accommodating himself to the ideas of the company; and he never spoke on his own views, unless he was asked about them. But if he noticed that any one asked him impertinent questions, intended to make sport of him, he immediately gave such an*

> *answer that the questioner was obliged to keep silence.* [80]

The situation in his native Sweden was more complicated. Here, too, he had disciples; there were two in particular, Johan Rosén and Gabriel Beyer, both of them teachers. Swedenborg always preferred to write in Latin, thus obscuring his beliefs from vulgar eyes. But Rosén reprinted a German review of his *The Apocalypse Revealed*, originally published in 1766, and Beyer had published a book concerning Swedenborg's doctrines entitled *New Attempts at Explaining The Texts for Sundays and Holidays* or, more succinctly, *Household Sermons*. Both had been published in Swedish, but later came under the scrutiny of the religious authorities.

Swedenborg himself was too honoured and illustrious to face persecution, as no doubt he realized, but the two men were not in that fortunate position. The Gothenburg Consistory, made up of the more prominent Lutheran

clergy and the local bishop, declared that the
teachings promulgated by the two men were
opposed to Lutheran doctrine and were too
close to Socinianism. Socinians, who became
known as the 'Polish Brethren' at the end of
the seventeenth century, rejected the divinity of
Christ and thus the existence of the Trinity. The
dean of the Consistory, Olof A Ekebom, published
these conclusions, which were repudiated by
Swedenborg in a strongly worded letter. The
dean then referred the matter to the House of
Clergy, one of the four divisions of parliament,
who decreed that Rosén and Beyer should appear
before the king to explain their aberrations and
false doctrines.

They defended themselves against the
accusations, and Swedenborg wrote them letters
of encouragement. Nevertheless the royal council
took away Beyer's appointment as teacher and
warned Rosén to refrain from mentioning
Swedenborg to his students. Swedenborg in turn
wrote to the king in order to protest against these

measures. In 1771 the whole matter was then referred to the Appeals Court, where it lingered for four years in legal limbo.

Eventually it was decided to refer the controversy to the senior scholars of Uppsala University, by which time Rosén had died and Beyer was allowed to resume teaching. But there were still people who vehemently opposed Swedenborg. A group planned to ensure that he was declared insane, whereupon Swedenborg fell upon his knees in his garden and asked for divine help and advice; he was comforted by the illumination that all would be well.[81]

On another occasion a young man came to his house with the intention of assassinating him, but snagged his coat on a nail, dropping his sword in the process; he snatched up his sword and ran away.[82]

*

Swedenborg himself was still writing, with the publication of *The Interaction of the Soul*

& Body in 1769 and of *The True Christian Religion* in 1771. These were essentially restatements of his original themes, but in *The Interaction* he describes what must have been one of his final visions; he had prayed that he might converse with the followers of Leibniz, Aristotle and Descartes on the subject of the soul's relation with the body. Nine men appeared in a vision, three from each faction, but then behind them he discerned three figures crowned with laurel. He knew at once that they were the three renowned philosophers themselves who had come to manage the debate. It was all courteous and polite until a spirit ascended with a torch in his right hand, which he shook before the faces of the nine men; the men then fell into dispute and argument.

The same spirit appeared again, with the torch in his left hand which he shook behind their heads. Whereupon the men became confused, and did not know whether to assert the primacy of spiritual influx, physical influx or pre-established harmony. They decided to choose by lot, and of course spiritual influx was drawn out.[83]

An angel then appeared and told them that they had made their choice not by chance but by divine providence. In the inside cover of his own copy of *The True Christian Religion* he wrote down the gifts that heaven had bestowed upon him. They included 'A beautiful red chest, consisting of 5 compartments [. . .] A beautiful shirt—a beautiful cap [. . .] A small crown set with 5 diamonds, which is worn in heaven on the side of the head'.[84] There were thirteen gifts in all, but it is not known if they ever took a physical presence.

In August 1771 he travelled once again to London, which had grown more and more congenial to him. Here he discussed with his English followers the translation of all his works. During that December, however, he suffered a stroke which, to his dismay, significantly impaired his spiritual faculties. That visionary

sight was restored but he remained partially
paralysed and explained to those around him
that his life in the world would soon cease. There
was one person, however, whom he still wanted to
meet. In February 1772 he wrote to John Wesley,
the founder of the Methodist movement. 'Sir, — I
have been informed in the world of spirits that
you have a strong desire to converse with me; I
shall be happy to see you, if you will favour me
with a visit'.[85]

Wesley was astonished by the letter, since he
had told no one about his wish to talk with
Swedenborg. He replied that he could not see
him yet because he was about to embark on a
six-month journey. Swedenborg replied that this
would be impossible as he was preparing himself
to enter the spiritual world 'on the 29th day of
the next month'.[86]

On the afternoon of 29 March Swedenborg
lay in the bed of his lodgings, with only the
landlady and housemaid for company. He had
rented rooms from a barber and wigmaker in

26 Great Bath Street in Clerkenwell, Richard Shearsmith; this was his favoured district. He knew very well that he was dying and his old friend, Ferelius, administered Holy Communion to him. It was a Sunday, and the church bells were ringing. He asked the women for the time, and they replied that it was five o'clock. 'Dat be good', he said, 'me tank you, God bless you'.[87] Ten minutes later he sighed and gave up his spirit. He was eighty-four years old. He was buried close by, in a vault under the Swedish Church in Princes Square, Wapping; this is just north of the Thames and close to the Danish Church in Wellclose Square, a square in which he had once lodged. The first stone of the Swedish Church was laid in 1728.

Curiously enough, the original Swedish congregation, formed in 1710, had asked for the help and advice of Swedenborg's father, Jesper Swedberg. The funeral service was conducted by Ferelius himself. Swedenborg's body was exhumed in 1908, and was removed to Uppsala Cathedral

where it remains. The Swedish church was closed
three years later, in 1911, and the area slowly
redeveloped; it was renamed as Swedenborg
Square in 1938, and can still be visited, today
called Swedenborg Gardens.

Swedenborg himself survived in the spirit and,
within a few years of his death, many hundreds
of people had assembled to conduct services
according to his teachings. In London a disciple,
Robert Hindmarsh, began a series of readings at
his house in Clerkenwell; in 1787, Hindmarsh's
brethren organized their first public religious
service. Soon enough they rented a chapel in
Great East Cheap which became known as the
New Jerusalem Church.

The New Church was then established in other
places since, as Hindmarsh wrote:

*The Church was now spreading itself in
many towns and villages, where heretofore
the doctrines had been unknown; and
in several places public worship was*

instituted, as soon as rooms or meeting-houses could be engaged for that purpose. [88]

The Swedenborg Society, established in 1810, is now in the heart of London. The English example was followed in the United States and in Canada, in Europe and in Africa. The inspiration of this remarkable visionary has never faded.

Endnotes

1   Lars Bergquist, *Swedenborg's Secret* (London: Swedenborg Society, 2005), p. 4.

2   Emanuel Swedenborg, *Conjugial Love*, tr. John Chadwick (London: Swedenborg Society, 1996), §395, p. 376.

3   Swedenborg, letter to Gabriel Beyer, 14 November 1769, quoted in Bergquist, *Swedenborg's Secret*, p. 294.

4   Swedenborg, letter to Eric Benzelius, 9 August 1715, quoted in Bergquist, *Swedenborg's Secret*, p. 57.

5   Swedenborg, *The Principia*, tr. Augustus Clissold, 2 vols. (London: W Newbery, 1845-6), vol. I, p. 50.

6   Swedenborg, *Arcana Caelestia*, tr. John Elliott, 12 vols. (London: Swedenborg Society, 1983-99), vol. 1, §775.2, p. 289.

7   Bergquist, *Swedenborg's Secret*, p. 117; cf. David Dunér, 'Swedenborg's Spiral', in *Studia*

Swedenborgiana, vol. 12, no. 4 (October 2002), p. 7.

8   Swedenborg, *The Principia*, vol. I, p. 35.

9   See Swedenborg, *Angelic Wisdom concerning the Divine Love and Wisdom*, tr. Clifford and Doris H Harley (London: Swedenborg Society, 1987), §§362-6, pp. 156-9 and *On the Divine Love—On the Divine Wisdom*, tr. E C Mongredien (London: Swedenborg Society, 1986), §86, pp. 90-1.

10   Lars Bergquist, *Swedenborg's Dream Diary*, tr. Anders Hallengren (West Chester, PA: Swedenborg Foundation, 2001), p. 316.

11   Swedenborg, *Arcana Caelestia*, vol. 1, §1001.3, p. 410.

12   Ibid., vol. 4, §2991, p. 51.

13   R L Tafel (tr., ed. and comp.), *Documents Concerning the Life and Character of Emanuel Swedenborg*, 3 vols. (London: Swedenborg Society, 1875-7), vol. I, p. 9.

14   Swedenborg, *Swedenborg's Journal of Dreams 1743-1744*, tr. J J G Wilkinson, ed. William Ross Woofenden, 2nd edn. (London: Swedenborg Society and Bryn Athyn, PA: Swedenborg Scientific Association, 1989), p. 49.

15   Bergquist, *Swedenborg's Dream Diary*, p. 126.

16   Ibid.

17   Ibid., p. 55.

18 Swedenborg, *Swedenborg's Journal of Dreams 1743-1744*, p. 96.

19 Swedenborg, *The Spiritual Diary*, tr. W H Acton and A W Acton (London: Swedenborg Society, 2002), vol. 1, §397, p. 123.

20 Tafel (tr., ed. and comp.), *Documents*, vol. I, pp. 35-6.

21 Christian de Tuxen, 'Testimony', in Carl Robsahm, *Memoirs of Swedenborg and other documents*, tr. and introd. Anders Hallengren (London: Swedenborg Society, 2011), p. 112.

22 Bergquist, *Swedenborg's Dream Diary*, pp. 295, 313; Bergquist, *Swedenborg's Secret*, pp. 173-4.

23 Tafel (tr., ed. and comp.), *Documents*, vol. II:2, p. 710.

24 Swedenborg, *The Worship and Love of God*, §55, quoted in Bergquist, *Swedenborg's Secret*, p. 179.

25 Samuel Taylor Coleridge, annotation of Swedenborg's *De Cultu et Amore Dei* (1745), dated 22 September 1821, quoted in 'Coleridge's View of Swedenborg', in *New Jerusalem Magazine* (Boston, MA: Otis Clapp), no. CLXVIII (August 1841), p. 474.

26 Swedenborg, *The Spiritual Diary*, §2060, quoted in Bergquist, *Swedenborg's Secret*, p. 184.

27 Swedenborg, *The Worship of Love and God*, §§57 ff., quoted in Bergquist, *Swedenborg's Secret*, p. 185.

28 Swedenborg, *The Worship of Love and God*, §86, quoted in Bergquist, *Swedenborg's Secret*, p. 189.

29 Swedenborg, *The Word of the Old Testament Explained*, §1003, quoted in George F Dole, 'Swedenborg's Modes of Presentation, 1745-1771', in Jonathan S Rose, Stuart Shotwell and Mary Lou Bertucci (eds.), *Scribe of Heaven: Swedenborg's Life, Work, and Impact* (West Chester, PA: Swedenborg Foundation, 2005), p. 100.

30 Swedenborg, *The Word of the Old Testament Explained*, §475, quoted in Bergquist, *Swedenborg's Secret*, p. 209.

31 Swedenborg, *The Word of the Old Testament Explained*, §1150, quoted in Bergquist, *Swedenborg's Secret*, p. 209.

32 Tafel (tr., ed. and comp.), *Documents*, vol. II:2, p. 492.

33 Dole, 'Swedenborg's Modes of Presentation', p. 101.

34 Robsahm, *Memoirs of Swedenborg and other documents*, p. 1.

35 Ibid., p. 2.

36 Ibid., p. 4.

37 Ibid., p. 11.

38 Ibid., p. 12.

39 Ibid., p. 13.

40 Swedenborg, *Arcana Caelestia*, §127, vol. 1, p. 53.

41 Rev. 21:1-5, quoted in Bergquist, *Swedenborg's Secret*, p. 289.

42 Swedenborg, *Heaven and Its Wonders and Hell*, tr.

Doris H Harley (London: Swedenborg Society, 1992), §§1-2, p. 3.

43 Ibid., §§237, 236, pp. 113, 112.

44 Ibid., §13, p. 8.

45 Ibid., §241, p. 115.

46 Swedenborg, *Heaven and Hell*, tr. George F Dole (New York: Swedenborg Foundation, 1984), §239, pp. 172-3.

47 Ibid., §240, p. 173.

48 Swedenborg, *Heaven and Its Wonders and Hell*, tr. Doris H Harley, §52, p. 24.

49 Ibid., §59, p. 28.

50 Ibid., §75, p. 35.

51 Ibid., §§96-7, p. 47.

52 Ibid., §110, p. 53.

53 Gary Lachman, *Into the Interior: Discovering Swedenborg* (London: Swedenborg Society, 2009), p. 122.

54 Swedenborg, *Heaven and Its Wonders and Hell*, tr. Doris H Harley, §184, p. 89.

55 Ibid., §184, p. 89.

56 Ibid., §488, p. 271.

57 Ibid., §§541, 543, p. 308.

58 Ibid., §547, p. 311.

59 Ibid., §548, p. 311.

60 Ibid., §574, p. 327.

61 Ibid., §553, pp. 314-15.

62 Ibid., §569, p. 324.

63 Ibid., §584, p. 333.

64 Ibid., §586, pp. 334-5.

65 Swedenborg, *On the New Jerusalem and Heaven's Teaching for It*, tr. John Chadwick (London: Swedenborg Society, 1990), §269, p. 92.

66 Swedenborg, *Other Planets*, tr. George F Dole and Jonathan S Rose (West Chester, PA: Swedenborg Foundation, 2018), §§52, 6, 11, 22, pp. 29, 6-8, 12.

67 Ibid., §111, p. 64.

68 Swedenborg, *Angelic Wisdom concerning the Divine Love and Wisdom*, §§11, 371, pp. 5, 161.

69 Swedenborg, *Marriage Love*, §522, quoted in Dole, 'Swedenborg's Modes of Presentation', p. 110.

70 Tafel (tr., ed. and comp.), *Documents*, vol. II:1, p. 629.

71 Cyriel Odhner Sigstedt, *The Swedenborg Epic: The Life and Works of Emanuel Swedenborg* (London: Swedenborg Society, 1981), p. 278.

72 Quoted in Christian de Tuxen, 'Testimony', in Robsahm, *Memoirs of Swedenborg and other documents*, p. 109.

73 Tafel (tr., ed. and comp.), *Documents*, vol. II:1, p. 660.

74 Swedenborg, *Marriage Love*, §155, quoted in Richard Smoley, 'The Inner Journey of Emanuel Swedenborg', in Rose et al. (eds.), *Scribe of Heaven*, p. 42.

75 Swedenborg, *The Apocalypse Explained*, tr. Isaiah Tansley, 6 vols. (London: Swedenborg Society, 1980-99), vol. V, §1000.4, p. 435.

76 Ibid., §1000.5, p. 436.

77 Swedenborg, *The Delights of Wisdom concerning Conjugial Love*, tr. Alfred Acton (London: Swedenborg Society, 1989), §76.6, p. 74.

78 Robsahm, *Memoirs of Swedenborg and other documents*, p. 16.

79 G W Carlson, 'Anteckningar, &c. Notices respecting the Swedish Church in London', in *The Monthly Observer and New Church Record* (London), vol. V, no. LI (1 March 1861), p. 89.

80 Tafel (tr., ed. and comp.), *Documents*, vol. II:1, p. 560.

81 Robsahm, *Memoirs of Swedenborg and other documents*, pp. 21-2.

82 Smoley, 'The Inner Journey of Emanuel Swedenborg', p. 45; Tafel (tr., ed. and comp.), *Documents*, vol. I, pp. 59-60.

83 Swedenborg, *Regarding the Interaction of Soul and Body*, tr. John Elliott (London: Swedenborg Society, 2012), §19, pp. 63-7.

84 Bergquist, *Swedenborg's Secret*, p. 414.

85 Tafel (tr., ed. and comp.), *Documents*, vol. II:1, p. 565.

86 Ibid.

87 Ibid., p. 578.

88 Robert Hindmarsh, *Rise and Progress of the New Jerusalem Church*, ed. Edward Madeley (London: Hodson & Son, 1861), p. 200.

Swedenborg: select works

— OTHER TITLES —

On the Conjugial Angel

A S Byatt

'. . . one of Britain's foremost grandes dames of the
writing world' —*The Sunday Telegraph*

Drawn from the transcript of a talk given at Swedenborg
House in 2010, *On the Conjugial Angel* explores
Swedenborg's influence on literature, the lives of the
Tennysons, the conflict between religion and science
and offers an intimate insight into A S Byatt's writing
methods. It is the sixth volume in the Swedenborg
Archive Series.

A S BYATT has written numerous works of fiction
including *Possession: A Romance* (1990), for
which she won the Booker Prize; *Angels and Insects*
(1992) and *The Children's Book* (2009). She was
made a Fellow of University College London in 2004
and a Fellow of the British Academy in 2017.

www.swedenborg.org.uk/books

www.swedenborg.org.uk/books

Introducing Swedenborg: Correspondences

Gary Lachman

'Lachman writes about philosophical and mystical ideas with exceptional grace, forcefulness and clarity'—*Washington Post*

Swedenborg today is acknowledged as one of the great thinkers of the eighteenth century and a pioneering figure in the history of Western thought. *Introducing Swedenborg: Correspondences* is the second in a series of pocket introductions providing accessible essays on key themes and works.

GARY LACHMAN is the author of many books on a range of esoteric, literary and countercultural themes. For the Swedenborg Society he has written *Into the Interior: Discovering Swedenborg* (2009) which was republished by Tarcher as *Swedenborg: an Introduction to his Life and Ideas* (2012).

www.swedenborg.org.uk/books